Macmillan/McGraw-Hill Science

Earth rotates as it revolves around the sun

A SYSTEM IN THE SKY

Authors

Mary Atwater
The University of Georgia

Prentice Baptiste
University of Houston

Lucy Daniel
Rutherford County Schools

Jay Hackett
University of Northern Colorado

Richard Moyer
University of Michigan, Dearborn

Carol Takemoto
Los Angeles Unified School District

Nancy Wilson
Sacramento Unified School District

Macmillan/McGraw-Hill School Publishing Company
New York   Columbus

MACMILLAN / McGRAW-HILL

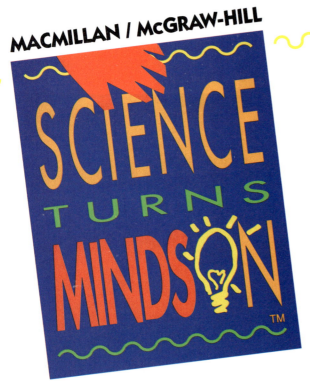

CONSULTANTS

Assessment:

Janice M. Camplin
Curriculum Coordinator, Elementary Science
Mentor, Western New York
Lake Shore Central Schools
Angola, NY

Mary Hamm
Associate Professor
Department of Elementary Education
San Francisco State University
San Francisco, CA

Cognitive Development:

Dr. Elisabeth Charron
Assistant Professor of Science Education
Montana State University
Bozeman, MT

Sue Teele
Director of Education Extension
University of California, Riverside
Riverside, CA

Cooperative Learning:

Harold Pratt
Executive Director of Curriculum
Jefferson County Public Schools
Golden, CO

Earth Science:

Thomas A. Davies
Research Scientist
The University of Texas
Austin, TX

David G. Futch
Associate Professor of Biology
San Diego State University
San Diego, CA

Dr. Shadia Rifai Habbal
Harvard-Smithsonian Center for Astrophysics
Cambridge, MA

Tom Murphree, Ph.D.
Global Systems Studies
Monterey, CA

Suzanne O'Connell
Assistant Professor
Wesleyan University
Middletown, CT

Environmental Education:

Cheryl Charles, Ph.D.
Executive Director
Project Wild
Boulder, CO

Gifted:

Sandra N. Kaplan
Associate Director, National/State Leadership
Training Institute on the Gifted/Talented
Ventura County Superintendent of Schools Office
Northridge, CA

Global Education:

M. Eugene Gilliom
Professor of Social Studies and Global Education
The Ohio State University
Columbus, OH

Merry M. Merryfield
Assistant Professor of Social Studies and Global Education
The Ohio State University
Columbus, OH

Intermediate Specialist

Sharon L. Strating
Missouri State Teacher of the Year
Northwest Missouri State University
Marysville, MO

Life Science:

Carl D. Barrentine
Associate Professor of Biology
California State University
Bakersfield, CA

V.L. Holland
Professor and Chair, Biological Sciences Department
California Polytechnic State University
San Luis Obispo, CA

Donald C. Lisowy
Education Specialist
New York, NY

Dan B. Walker
Associate Dean for Science Education and Professor of Biology
San Jose State University
San Jose, CA

Literature:

Dr. Donna E. Norton
Texas A&M University
College Station, TX

Tina Thoburn, Ed.D.
President
Thoburn Educational Enterprises, Inc.
Ligonier, PA

Copyright © 1995 Macmillan/McGraw-Hill School Publishing Company

All rights reserved. No part of this book may be reproduced or transmitted in any form or by any means, electronic or mechanical, including photocopying, recording, or by any information storage and retrieval system, without permission in writing from the publisher.

Macmillan/McGraw-Hill School Division
10 Union Square East
New York, New York 10003

Printed in the United States of America

ISBN 0-02-276111-X/3

3 4 5 6 7 8 9 VHJ 99 98 97 96 95

The moon

Mathematics:
Martin L. Johnson
Professor, Mathematics Education
University of Maryland at College Park
College Park, MD

Physical Science:
Max Diem, Ph.D.
Professor of Chemistry
City University of New York, Hunter College
New York, NY

Gretchen M. Gillis
Geologist
Maxus Exploration Company
Dallas, TX

Wendell H. Potter
Associate Professor of Physics
Department of Physics
University of California, Davis
Davis, CA

Claudia K. Viehland
Educational Consultant, Chemist
Sigma Chemical Company
St. Louis, MO

Reading:
Jean Wallace Gillet
Reading Teacher
Charlottesville Public Schools
Charlottesville, VA

Charles Temple, Ph. D.
Associate Professor of Education
Hobart and William Smith Colleges
Geneva, NY

Safety:
Janice Sutkus
Program Manager: Education
National Safety Council
Chicago, IL

Science Technology and Society (STS):
William C. Kyle, Jr.
Director, School Mathematics and Science Center
Purdue University
West Lafayette, IN

Social Studies:
Mary A. McFarland
Instructional Coordinator of Social Studies, K-12, and Director of Staff Development
Parkway School District
St. Louis, MO

Students Acquiring English:
Mrs. Bronwyn G. Frederick, M.A.
Bilingual Teacher
Pomona Unified School District
Pomona, CA

Misconceptions:
Dr. Charles W. Anderson
Michigan State University
East Lansing, MI

Dr. Edward L. Smith
Michigan State University
East Lansing, MI

Multicultural:
Bernard L. Charles
Senior Vice President
Quality Education for Minorities Network
Washington, DC

Cheryl Willis Hudson
Graphic Designer and Publishing Consultant
Part Owner and Publisher, Just Us Books, Inc.
Orange, NJ

Paul B. Janeczko
Poet
Hebron, MA

James R. Murphy
Math Teacher
La Guardia High School
New York, NY

Ramon L. Santiago
Professor of Education and Director of ESL
Lehman College, City University of New York
Bronx, NY

Clifford E. Trafzer
Professor and Chair, Ethnic Studies
University of California, Riverside
Riverside, CA

STUDENT ACTIVITY TESTERS

Jennifer Kildow
Brooke Straub
Cassie Zistl
Betsy McKeown
Seth McLaughlin
Max Berry
Wayne Henderson

FIELD TEST TEACHERS

Sharon Ervin
San Pablo Elementary School
Jacksonville, FL

Michelle Gallaway
Indianapolis Public School #44
Indianapolis, IN

Kathryn Gallman
#7 School
Rochester, NY

Karla McBride
#44 School
Rochester, NY

Diane Pease
Leopold Elementary
Madison, WI

Kathy Perez
Martin Luther King Elementary
Jacksonville, FL

Ralph Stamler
Thoreau School
Madison, WI

Joanne Stern
Hilltop Elementary School
Glen Burnie, MD

Janet Young
Indianapolis Public School #90
Indianapolis, IN

CONTRIBUTING WRITER

Fred Schroyer

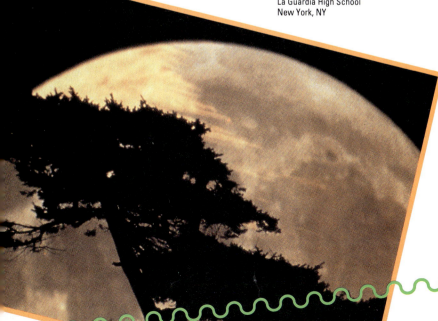

A System in the Sky

Lessons   Themes

Unit Introduction   A System in the Sky .... **Systems and Interactions** **6**
What do the sun, Earth, and moon have in common with a bike? More than you think!

1 How Does Earth Move? .... **Models** **12**
Take a trip through time, and collect the evidence to solve one of Earth's oldest mysteries.

2 Can You Trust Your Eyes About Size? .... **Scale and Structure** **26**
Discover why seeing is not always believing.

3 Do Earth and the Moon Cast Shadows? .... **Systems and Interactions** **36**
If shadows have to fall on something to be seen, what do they fall on in space?

4 Why Does the Moon Change? .... **Patterns of Change** **48**
Now, you see it. Now, you don't. What's really happening to the moon?

5 How Are Earth and the Moon Different? ... **Scale and Structure** **58**
The moon may be a nice place to visit, but Earth makes a better "Home, Sweet Home."

6 Are There Reasons for the Seasons? .... **Energy** **70**
Is your summer in January or July? It depends on where you live.

Unit Wrap Up   Your Solar Neighborhood .... **Systems and Interactions** **80**
When it comes to your solar neighborhood, you have to learn to think BIG! Find out why your address doesn't end with your zip code.

Activities!

EXPLORE

Why Is There Day and Night? 14
Take a Closer Look 28
Shadow Games in Space 38
The Pattern of the Moon 50
**How Can You Make
Moon Craters?** 60
Why Is it Warmer in Summer? 72

TRY THIS

Project Moonwatch! 9
How Many Days and Nights? 21
A Telescope for Both Eyes 23
How Big Is Big? 31
It's Farther Than You Think! 33
How Can You Measure the Moon? 34
You Can View the Sun 45
Mission Accomplished 53
Earth Phases? 57
Footprints Forever? 65
Where Is It Summer? 76
How Many Hours? 76

Features

Links

Social **S**tudies **L**ink
Observing the Sky 17
What Time Is It? 47

Math **L**ink
A Long Walk 31
Your Age in Orbits 53
What's Your Moon Weight? 67

Literature **L**ink
Science in Literature 10
The Sun by Seymour Simon 67
Shadow Puppets 82

Music/**A**rt **L**ink
Your Own Space Suit 69

Health **L**ink
Watch Out for UV! 78

CAREERS

Picture Perfect (Animator) 24

SCIENCE TECHNOLOGY and Society

Starlight, Starbright 25

Focus on **E**nvironment
Taking Care of Earth 78

Focus on **T**echnology
Coming Home 63
Moontown? 69

Departments

Glossary 84
Index 86
Credits 88

Theme T SYSTEMS and INTERACTIONS

A System in the Sky

What are the sun, Earth, and the moon made of? How do they move? What do they really look like? People have been thinking about these questions for a long, long time. They have told stories, sung songs, painted pictures, and written books to answer these questions. All of these are ways of knowing.

What do you know about the sun, Earth, and the moon? Have you ever thought about any of these questions? Do you have some questions of your own?

Where does the sun go at night?

When the sun sets over an ocean or a lake, does it sink right down into the water and make it boil? How do you know?

How can Earth be round when it looks so flat?

If you dug a really deep hole, would you come out on the other side of the world?

What is the moon made of, anyway? Sometimes, it looks orange or yellow. Other times, it's pale green or white.

Does the moon have a face? Did a cow really jump over the moon, as it says in the nursery rhyme?

This book is another way to find out about our Earth, the sun, and the moon. In some ways, they're different. One of them is our home. One gives us heat and light. And one is our nearest neighbor. In another way, they're alike. They're all part of the same system (sis′ təm).

A **system** is a group of things that work together. A bicycle is a system. Its wheels, gears, and chain all work together. When you pedal, the gears and chain drive one wheel. What happens if you take away a wheel or the gears or the chain? The bike doesn't work as it did before. The system has changed.

This book will help you understand what the sun, Earth, and the moon each do in their system. You'll learn about how it works.

Science is a way of knowing and learning. Scientists try to learn about things by observing them and asking questions. Next, they think up answers to the questions based on what they have observed. Then, they test their answers by doing experiments.

Take the moon, for example. For hundreds of years, scientists have been thinking about the question, what is the moon like? So, what did they do? They observed it. They studied it through telescopes. They did experiments.

Astronaut on the moon

Scientists using sextant to observe stars

In this century, scientists have taken pictures of the moon. They sent spacecraft without people to study conditions there. Then they sent astronauts to the moon to get samples of it.

As scientists gather more and more information, they change many of their ideas about the moon. This is how science works. Scientists continue to change their ideas and explanations as they discover new information.

In the next activity, you'll be observing the moon to help you think about a question that people have been asking for thousands of years.

Project Moonwatch!

What You Need
Activity Log page 1

Does the moon change shape in the sky? A calendar on page 1 in your **Activity Log** has places where you can draw what the moon looks like. Every night for two weeks, look at the moon and draw what you see. Ask a grown-up to help you. If it's cloudy some nights and you can't see the moon, don't worry. Just leave those places blank. You will use your observations later on in this unit.

Literature  Link

Science in Literature

Here are some books that tell you more about Earth, the sun, and the moon. If you have questions, you'll find plenty of answers in them.

The Truth About the Moon by Clayton Bess. Boston: Houghton Mifflin Company, 1983.

Sumu was a very curious little boy. He kept asking different people in his West African village about the moon, and he got some wonderful answers. But they were all different!

When you read this book, look for all the different answers to Sumu's questions. Think about what you would say if he asked you. Later in this unit, read the book again. Compare the information about the moon in this book with the story. What do you think is the truth about the moon?

The Sun by Seymour Simon.
New York: Mulberry Books, 1986.

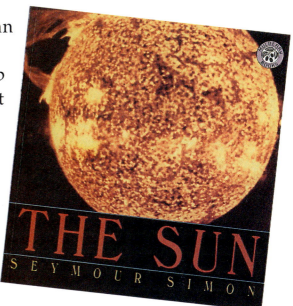

If the moon is a question, the sun is an exclamation! It's too bright to look at without hurting your eyes. It can keep you warm, but it can also dry things out and burn things up. Seymour Simon's book *The Sun* tells how big it is, how hot it is, what it's made of, and much more. Photographs let you see the sun up close. Drawings help you understand about its place in space.

Read this book to look for new information. Talk with a friend who has read it. Compare the parts that had the most new information for each of you.

Other Good Books To Read

My Place in Space by Robin and Sally Hirst. New York: Orchard Books, 1988.

When Henry Wilson, a young Australian, is asked where he lives, his answer includes his solar system and even beyond.

Sunshine Makes the Seasons by Franklyn M. Branley. New York: Thomas Y. Crowell, 1985.

This book is a mixture of interesting examples and experiments about seasons.

The Orphan Boy by Tololwa M. Mollel. New York: Clarion Books, 1990.

This legend explains why the planet Venus is known to the Maasai (Mä sī′) of Kenya and Tanzania as the orphan boy.

Theme MODELS

HOW DOES EARTH MOVE?

*The night has a thousand eyes,
And the day but one;
Yet the light of the bright world dies
With the dying sun.*
    —Francis William Bourdillon

Photo collage of a sunrise

People have always watched the sun and moon and wondered how they move. Some people made up folk tales to explain the movements. Other people called astronomers (ə stron′ ə mərz) also carefully observed the sun and moon. Astronomers are scientists who study the sun, moon, planets, stars, and other objects in the sky. They saw the same things happen again and again. They used this information to explain scientifically what they saw.

Minds On! Try thinking like an astronomer. Draw the sun, Earth, and the moon in your *Activity Log* on page 2. Draw arrows to show how you think each moves.

EXPLORE Activity!

Why Is There Day and Night?

Like an astronomer, you can make models of the sun and Earth. Models help you understand how things work. You can use them to understand something that is too large or too small to see. Models are also useful when something is happening too fast or too slowly for you to observe. You can't take a trip out into space to observe how the sun and Earth are moving. But you know that the sun is the source of light for day. With models, you can explore what the sun and Earth do to cause day and night.

What You Need

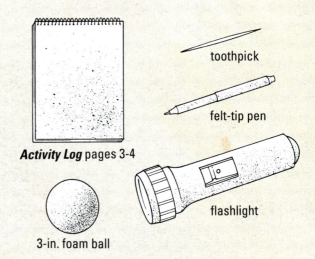

Activity Log pages 3-4

toothpick
felt-tip pen
flashlight
3-in. foam ball

What To Do

1 Stick the toothpick just far enough into the foam ball so you can use it as a handle.

2 With the marker, make a dot in the middle of the ball. The ball will be Earth in your model. The flashlight will be the sun in your model.

3 Hold the flashlight so that the light is shining toward the ceiling. Hold the ball by the toothpick, moving the ball to make light shine on the dot. If the flashlight is the sun and the ball is Earth, would it be day or night at the dot? Is it day or night on the other side of the ball?

4 With your group, think of two different ways to make day and night at the dot. Record your ideas in your *Activity Log.*

5 Make a model of each of your ideas, using the ball and the flashlight. Record your observations for each model in your *Activity Log.*

What Happened?

1. In the first model, what is moving? How did that movement cause day and night at the dot?
2. In the second model, what is moving? How did that movement cause day and night at the dot?

What Now?

1. Imagine that you are standing on the dot. How does the sun's position seem to change from where you are on the dot as you make night happen in each model?
2. Compare the models your group thought of with the models of other groups. Of all the models, which do you think best explains what you know about day and night? Why?
3. Look at your drawings on page 2 of the *Activity Log.* How would you change them?

Looking Ahead

You just used models to see why there is day and night. You will use models later in this unit to learn about eclipses (i klip′ sez) of the sun and moon. You will also use them to see why the moon seems to change and why we have seasons.

EXPLORE

How Earth Moves

In the activity, you used models to explore why there is day and night. Did you have trouble deciding which model was the best? For thousands of years, astronomers had the same trouble. We now know that Earth has day and night because of the way Earth moves.

Earth rotates (rō′ tāts) or spins once in each 24-hour day. It is night when your place on Earth is facing away from the sun. Day comes when your place on Earth faces the sun. In the activity, did you rotate Earth in one of your models to explain day and night?

Illustration not drawn to scale.

Minds On! What part of Earth is in daytime in this picture? What part is in nighttime?

But rotating is not the only way Earth moves. As it rotates, it also **revolves** (ri volvs′) or moves in a circle around the sun.

Observing the Sky

People have been trying to explain day and night for a long time. They watched the sun and moon move across the sky. They wondered where the sun went at night and why the moon changed shape.

In New Mexico, Native Americans carved a calendar into rock based on the movements of the sun, Earth, and the moon. In Mexico and Peru, people built large stone buildings called **observatories** (əb zûr′ və tôr′ ēz) to watch how the sun and moon moved.

In other parts of the world, people placed large stones in patterns. The stones lined up with the sun or moon on days like the first day of summer. Scientists find these stones today in England, France, and Kenya.

Use a map of the world to find each of these places. It will help you to see that people everywhere were thinking about our place in space.

Stone patterns in northwest Kenya

For a long time, no one knew that Earth revolves around the sun. They thought the sun revolved around Earth. In fact, astronomers have been working on this problem for 2,000 years. The ideas of many people from all over the world have added pieces to the puzzle.

1 About 300 B.C., Zhou Yue (jō′ yüe′) from China made a model of how the moon moves.

2 Around A.D. 150, Ptolemy (tol′ ə mē), while living in Egypt, made a model of how the sun, Earth, and the moon work together. He said that Earth is at the center of everything. In his model, the sun, moon, and stars all revolve around Earth.

3 About A.D. 400, Hypatia (hī pā′ shə), a mathematician in Alexandria, Egypt, developed an instrument that measured the positions of the stars and planets.

4 In 497, Aryabhata (är yä′ bä tä′) the First from India added his own idea. He said that Earth rotates.

5 During 880–909, Al-Battani (äl′ bä tä′ nē) from Turkey figured out the length of a year and the seasons. He also improved Ptolemy's model.

6 In 1543, a Polish astronomer, Nicolaus Copernicus (kə pûr′ ni kəs), made a different model. In it, the sun is at the center. Earth revolves around the sun, rotating as it goes.

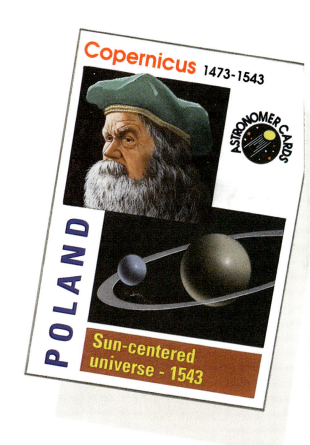

7 Galileo (gal′ ə lā′ ō) was an astronomer in Italy in the 1600s. He knew what other astronomers had said about the movements of the sun, Earth, and the moon. He also knew about an instrument called a **telescope** (tel′ ə skōp′) that makes faraway objects look brighter and clearer. He used a telescope he made to observe the sky.

One night in 1610, Galileo looked through his telescope at the planet Jupiter. He was amazed! He saw that Jupiter had four little moons that revolve around it. He watched the positions of the moons change each night as they moved around Jupiter.

So Galileo wondered. Could it be that Earth's moon travels around Earth in the same way? And could it be that Earth revolves around the sun in the same way? It turns out that Galileo was right!

Earth revolves around the sun in an orbit (ôr′ bit). An **orbit** is a path that an object follows as it revolves around another object. Earth takes one year to revolve all the way around the sun. That's 365 days and nights.

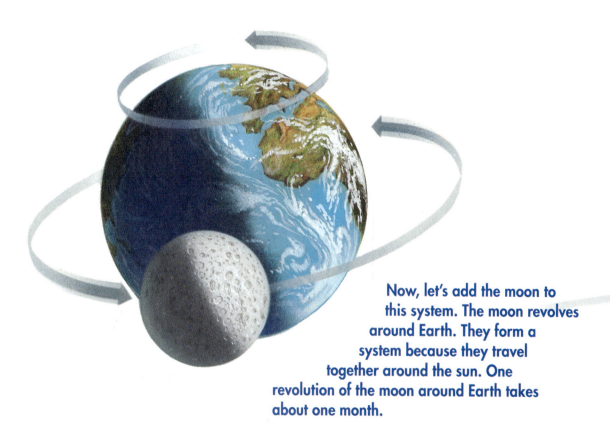

Now, let's add the moon to this system. The moon revolves around Earth. They form a system because they travel together around the sun. One revolution of the moon around Earth takes about one month.

Illustration not drawn to scale.

Minds On!

Remember how you made day and night happen in the Explore Activity? How many times does Earth rotate in one 24-hour day? How many times does Earth rotate in one year?

TRY THIS Activity!

How Many Days and Nights?

You can show how Earth rotates and revolves.

What You Need
foam ball with toothpick from the Explore Activity, light socket with cord and light bulb

Place the light in the middle of a table. **Safety Tip:** Put light bulb in socket before plugging it in. The light will be the sun in this model, and the ball will be Earth. Hold the ball so that the place you marked is facing the sun. Begin to rotate Earth making night and day. Continue to rotate Earth as you slowly move around the sun one time. How many times did Earth rotate as it revolved once around the sun? To make your model rotate as many times as Earth really does, the ball would have to rotate 365 times.

Seeing Better

We've learned much about the sun-Earth-moon system since Galileo's time. And astronomers today are still learning. Like the astronomers of the past, we learn many new things from using telescopes. Galileo used a simple telescope with glass lenses. **Lenses** are curved pieces of glass that bend light rays. They are like eyeglasses. The telescope Galileo used made objects look about 30 times closer than they really were. Today, telescopes used by astronomers can make objects look thousands of times closer than they really are.

Look through this to help you aim the telescope at an object.

Look through the eyepiece. It's a small lens that makes the object look closer and clearer.

This tripod holds the telescope still so it won't wiggle when you look through it.

We use telescopes to view things on Earth as well as in the sky. **Binoculars** (bə nok′ yə lərz) are two small telescopes connected side by side so you can look through one with each eye.

Binoculars

The light from the object travels through this tube to the eyepiece.

This is where light enters the telescope.
The bigger this lens is, the better you can see dim, faraway objects.

TRY THIS Activity!

A Telescope for Both Eyes

In this activity, you will observe an object twice and compare what you see.

What You Need
pair of binoculars, 2-in. foam ball, pencil, *Activity Log* page 5

To begin, use the pencil to make several small dents and marks on the ball. Place it in a corner of the room. Next, go to the opposite corner of the room. Observe the ball. Record your observations in your *Activity Log*. Now, observe it through binoculars. Record your observations. Compare your observations. Why do you think people use binoculars to observe birds and other animals? What are some other ways to use binoculars?

In addition to instruments like telescopes and binoculars, scientists have also used models and drawings. Today, they use moving pictures and computer art, too.

 ## Picture Perfect

If you like to draw, you might like to become an animator. An animator makes drawings and puts them together to make moving pictures. Cartoons are one example of the kind of work they do. But that's not all. Some animators make drawings and videos that scientists use to help people better understand important science ideas. They use animation when they can't take pictures of things that are very small or very big like the sun, Earth, and the moon. Sometimes they use computers to create the art. If you think you might like to become an animator, you'll need to go to college or art school to learn more about art. In the meantime, keep drawing!

Animator creating art on a computer

Even with the best instruments and models, astronomers can't work if they can't see objects in space clearly. Strange as it may seem, this is getting to be a big problem.

Skyglow as seen from space

SCIENCE TECHNOLOGY AND Society

Starlight, Starbright

Astronomers work mostly at night. The sun is so bright during the day that they can't see objects in the sky very well. Some objects, like stars, they can't see at all. But as Earth rotates, it grows dark and stars appear.

When you go outside at night, can you see the stars? If you live in a small town, you probably can. But in cities, the night sky is filled with light. It comes from thousands of lights that people use. This light is called **skyglow** (skī′ glō). Some skyglow is so bright it can be seen from space. Why might people call skyglow *light pollution*? Who might think it's a problem? How might we decrease light pollution in our cities?

Minds On! What other objects besides the sun, moon, and stars can you see in the sky? Can you see them better during the day or at night? ●

Sum It Up

People have always wondered about objects in the sky. Their observations helped them explain how these objects moved. As they observed, they changed their ideas. They learned that the moon revolves around Earth and that Earth revolves around the sun. As Earth rotates, there is day and night. Scientists use models, as you did, to explain how the sun, Earth, and the moon move.

Critical Thinking

1. How are rotating and revolving different?
2. If Earth rotated slower, would we have longer or shorter days?
3. How does having day and night affect plants, people, and other animals?

When an airplane is high in the sky, it looks small enough to put into your pocket. But if you've seen one on the ground, you know how big it is. Why do you think something that's so big looks so small when it's far away?

ABOUT SIZE?

Minds On! Put your pencil on the floor beside your desk and close one eye. Next, use your thumb and finger to "measure" the pencil. Now, lean down and compare your measurement with the real size of the pencil. Why do you think there's such a difference? ●

Your eyes tell you that the sun and moon are about the same size. Can you trust them? Find out in the next activity.

EXPLORE Activity!

Take a Closer Look

The sun and moon appear to be the same size in our sky. But one is actually larger. In this activity, you will use a model to explore why they look the same size when they're not.

What You Need

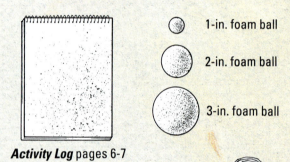

- 1-in. foam ball
- 2-in. foam ball
- 3-in. foam ball

Activity Log pages 6-7

meter tape or meter stick

notched index card

What To Do

1. Work in a small group. Place the 1-in. and 3-in. balls in a line across a table 10 cm from the edge. Bend down so your eyes are at table-top level. Look at the balls through the notch in the index card. Compare their sizes. Have each member of your group do this.

2 Leave the 1-in. ball where it is. Move the 3-in. ball back on the table until it appears to be the same size as the 1-in. ball. Measure the distance from the table edge to the 3-in. ball. Record this distance in your **Activity Log.**

3 Predict at what distance from the table edge you must place the 2-in. ball so that its size appears the same as the other balls. Record your prediction in your **Activity Log.** Then try it.

What Happened?

1. What did you observe as each ball moved farther from your eye?
2. Where did you place the 2-in. ball so that it appeared to be the same size as the other balls?
3. How did the locations of the three balls compare?

What Now?

1. Suppose you used a volleyball and a softball in this experiment. If you lined them up so that they appeared to be the same size, which one do you think would be farther away from you? Why?
2. The sun and moon appear to be the same size in our sky, but the sun is really much farther away from Earth. Using what you learned in the experiment, which of them do you think is larger? Why?

EXPLORE

How Big?

You learned in the Explore Activity that the farther away an object is, the smaller it looks. This is certainly true of the sun and moon. They are both big, but they look to be the size of basketballs in the sky because they are so far away.

Just like the balls you lined up in the Explore Activity, the sun and the moon appear to be the same size. That's because the sun is much farther away from Earth than the moon.

The sun is enormous. It is so big that if it were hollow, over one million Earths would fit inside it. Just because the sun is so large, that doesn't mean that the moon is small. The moon just looks small because it's so far away.

Sun　　　　　　　Moon

The sun is almost 400 times larger across than the moon. If you could walk around the sun without stopping, it would take you about 100 years.

The moon is one-fourth the size of Earth. If you could walk around the moon without stopping, it would take you about three months.

Earth is four times larger than the moon. In fact, the moon could almost fit into the Pacific Ocean. It would take you about 11 months to walk around Earth.

Illustration not drawn to scale.

TRY THIS Activity!

How Big Is Big?

You can compare the sizes of the sun, Earth, and the moon by making a model.

What You Need
piece of notebook paper, meter tape, masking tape, *Activity Log* page 8

In the center of the paper, draw a circle that is 1 cm across. This will be Earth. Now make a circle that is 2½ mm wide. This will be the moon. Then, use masking tape to make a circle on the floor that is 110 cm across. This will be the sun. Finally, put the notebook paper next to the circle on the floor. How do the moon and Earth compare in size to the sun? How do they compare in size to each other? Record your observations in your *Activity Log*.

Math Link

A Long Walk

If it would take you about 3 months to walk around the moon and about 11 months to walk around Earth, how many months would it take to walk around them both? Would that time be more than a year or less than a year?

31

How Far?

The sun looks small because it's very far away from Earth—150 million kilometers (93 million miles).

The sun is so far away that it takes eight minutes for sunlight to make the trip to Earth.

This picture shows how the sun and moon sometimes look to be the same size from Earth.

Light reflected from the moon reaches Earth in only 1¼ seconds. That's because the moon is much closer. It's about 385 thousand kilometers (240 thousand miles) from Earth.

Earth gets heat as well as light from the sun. It's a good thing we live at this distance from the sun. If we were much closer, Earth would be too hot to live on. And if we were much farther away, Earth would be too cold for living things.

Minds On! Suppose Earth moved farther from the sun. Would the sun appear larger or smaller in our sky? Suppose the moon moved closer to Earth. Would it appear larger or smaller than it does now? Why? Write what you think in your *Activity Log* on page 9.

TRY THIS Activity!

It's Farther Than You Think!

You can build a model of the sun-Earth-moon system to show how far they are from each other.

What You Need
3 pieces of paper, 3 craft sticks, masking tape, meter tape, *Activity Log* page 10

First, make three signs—sun, Earth, moon. Next, tape each sign to a stick. Now, go out to the school playground or a nearby park. Put the stick with the Earth sign into the ground at one end of the playground or park. Put the moon stick into the ground 38 cm away from the Earth stick. Measure 150 m from the Earth stick, and put the sun stick into the ground there. How do the moon and sun compare in their distance from Earth? Record your observations in your *Activity Log*.

Don't Trust Your Eyes

Minds On! Did you know that you can cover the moon with your thumb? When you see the moon in the sky, stretch out your arm, close one eye, and try it. Using what you've learned, explain in your *Activity Log* on page 11 how your thumb can cover up the moon.

Moon close to horizon

Here's another way your eyes play tricks on you. When a full moon is close to the horizon, it looks larger than when it is higher in the sky. But, it's always the same size. And you can prove it.

TRY THIS Activity!

How Can You Measure the Moon?

You can make an instrument to measure the moon.

What You Need
brass fastener, 2 paper shapes your teacher will give you, *Activity Log* page 11

First, match up the shapes. Next, gently push the brass fastener through the middle of the wide end of the shapes. Then, spread out the ends of the fastener to connect the shapes. Now, hold the instrument out at arm's length, and move the ends apart. Use this instrument to measure the full moon when it is on the horizon, and record the measurement. Then, measure again when the moon is higher in the sky. Record the measurement. Are they the same?

Moon higher in the sky

Minds On! Imagine you're on the moon, looking back at Earth. How big would Earth look? On page 12 in your *Activity Log*, draw a picture of how big you think the sun and Earth would look from the moon. •

Why the moon appears to be larger on the horizon than when it's higher in the sky probably has to do with what's around it.

When it's on the horizon, you're seeing ground, trees, and buildings, too. The scene you're looking at has more things in it. That probably makes the moon look bigger.

When you see the moon higher in the sky, it seems to be in a less crowded place than it does on the horizon. It looks smaller. Of course, the moon is the same size no matter where it is.

Sum It Up

Can you trust your eyes when it comes to size? You have learned in this lesson that you can't. Faraway things look smaller than they really are. As we have better understood that, we have changed what we thought we knew about the sun and moon. We now know that the sun is much bigger and much farther away from Earth.

Critical Thinking

1. Why is it important for the sun's light to reach Earth?
2. Why do you think space explorers went to the moon rather than the sun?
3. Do you think the stars are closer or farther away than the sun? Why?

Theme **T** SYSTEMS and INTERACTIONS

DO EARTH AND THE MOON CAST SHADOWS?

Can you make a shadow over these words? Go ahead and try it. Hold your hand low over the page. The page gets darker, doesn't it? Do you know why?

Almost everything the sun shines on has a shadow. Buildings and trees have shadows. You have a shadow.

Minds On! Look at a window or the lights in the room. Hold your hand up to block the light. Did the light go away? Why can't you see it? ●

Just as your hand got between your eyes and the light, clouds, buildings, and trees get between you and the sun. They make shadows on you because they block sunlight.

In the next activity, you'll explore what making shadows and blocking sunlight have to do with some of the unusual happenings in our sky.

EXPLORE Activity!

Shadow Games in Space

You already know that Earth and the moon are parts of a system moving around the sun. In this activity, you will use a model to find out what happens when the moon moves between the sun and Earth. Then you will discover what happens when Earth moves between the sun and the moon.

What You Need

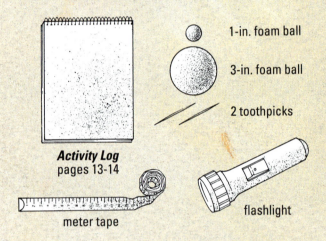

Activity Log pages 13-14
1-in. foam ball
3-in. foam ball
2 toothpicks
meter tape
flashlight

What To Do

1. Push a toothpick into each ball to make it easier to hold.

2. Work in a darkened room.

3. Predict where the shadow will fall if you hold the smaller ball between the light and the larger ball at a distance of 10 cm from the larger ball. Record your prediction.

4 Use the model to test your prediction. Record your observations, and compare them with your prediction.

5 Predict where the shadow will fall if you repeat the activity holding the larger ball between the light and the smaller ball at a distance of 10 cm from the larger ball. Record your prediction.

6 Use the model to test your prediction. Record your observations, and compare them with your prediction.

What Happened?

1. Compare your observations from steps 4 and 6.
2. Why did the shadows form?

What Now?

1. What does the larger ball represent? What does the smaller ball represent? What does the light represent?
2. What would you see if you were standing in the center of the shadow on the larger ball?

Lunar Eclipse

In the Explore Activity, you used a model to show that when the moon was between Earth and the sun, the moon's shadow fell on Earth. But the shadow didn't cover all of Earth. If you were standing in the center of the moon's shadow, you wouldn't see the sun. But if you were standing outside the shadow, you would. You also showed that when Earth was between the moon and the sun, Earth's shadow covered the whole moon.

When Earth moves between the moon and the sun, it's called a **lunar eclipse** (lü' nər i klips'). The moon moves through Earth's shadow and turns dark. Remember when you held your hand over the page and made a shadow? Your hand was doing what Earth does.

Both Earth and the moon always have a shadow. But you can't see their shadows. There just isn't anything out in space for them to fall on—except during an eclipse (i klips'). An **eclipse** is when one object passes into the shadow of another object.

Almost every year you can see a lunar eclipse somewhere in the United States. A lunar eclipse lasts an hour or two. Everyone on the side of Earth facing the moon may see a lunar eclipse as the moon moves into Earth's shadow.

Illustration not drawn to scale.

Solar Eclipse

When the moon moves between Earth and the sun, it's called a **solar eclipse** (sō′ lər i klips′). Earth moves through the moon's shadow, and part of Earth turns dark.

As you learned in Lesson 2, the moon happens to be just the right size and distance from Earth to make it look the same size as the sun. So when it moves directly between Earth and the sun during a solar eclipse, the moon blocks out the sunlight. Remember earlier in this lesson when you put your hand between your eyes and the light? Your hand was doing exactly what the moon does.

Because the moon is much smaller than Earth, its shadow covers only part of Earth's surface. That means that fewer people see solar eclipses than lunar eclipses.

42 Illustration not drawn to scale.

If you were in the darkest part of the moon's shadow during a solar eclipse, this is what you'd see from Earth.

Eclipses don't happen very often. The sun, Earth, and the moon usually don't line up in just the right way. When the moon orbits Earth, it usually misses going exactly between Earth and the sun. Because the moon's shadow misses Earth, there is no solar eclipse. And when the moon goes around the other side of Earth, it usually goes above or below Earth's shadow. So, there is no lunar eclipse.

Total and Partial Eclipses

When things do get lined up just right, it is a very impressive sight. In a total solar eclipse, the moon completely blocks out the sun for two to seven minutes, the time it takes for Earth and the moon to move out of line. The part of Earth in the moon's shadow gets so dark that some animals think it's night.

During a total solar eclipse, animals that are active during the day get ready to sleep. Those that sleep during the day may wake up and begin moving around.

Total solar eclipse

Owl with prey

In a partial solar eclipse, just part of the sun is blocked out. It's much less noticeable than a total eclipse because much of the sun's light is still visible.

There are total and partial eclipses of the moon, too. The moon doesn't become completely dark in most lunar eclipses.

Partial solar eclipse

Minds On!

Astronomers predict when eclipses will happen. Solar and lunar eclipses happen each year. On August 11, 1999, a total solar eclipse will be visible in Europe, the Middle East, and southern Asia. How old will you be then?

TRY THIS Activity!

You Can View the Sun

The sun's harmful rays can damage your eyes. Here's a way to view the sun safely.

What You Need
piece of black paper, piece of white paper, pin

Use the pin to punch a small hole in the center of the black paper. *Safety Tip:* Use the pin carefully. Put the white paper on the ground. Kneel beside it with your back to the sun. *Safety Tip:* Don't look directly at the sun. Hold the black paper above the white paper so a shadow is on the white paper. Move the black paper nearer to or farther from the white paper until the sun's image coming through the pinhole is clear.

How Science Works

Scientists build on each other's work. What was observed and discovered long ago is a base for today's scientists. And today's experiments will be a base for future scientists. Early astronomers in many different places studied eclipses and made scientific observations.

Early Chinese astronomers used sighting tubes to observe eclipses. Based on their observations, they predicted eclipses.

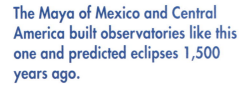

The Maya of Mexico and Central America built observatories like this one and predicted eclipses 1,500 years ago.

Today, scientists travel all over the world to study total solar eclipses. They can observe things about the sun that they can't observe as well at any other time.

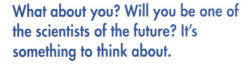

What about you? Will you be one of the scientists of the future? It's something to think about.

Social Studies Link

What Time Is It?

Before there were clocks, people used shadows to measure time. The shadow stick was invented about 5,500 years ago. As Earth rotated, the stick's shadow moved. People marked the place on the ground where the shadow fell.

A sundial is another way to measure time with shadows. It was invented about 3,000 years ago. Like the shadow stick, it measures the angle of the shadow cast by the sun. Both of these useful inventions were the result of people's study and observation of the sun.

Sundial

Sum It Up

Earth and the moon cast shadows as they move through space. When Earth or the moon moves through the other's shadow, we see an eclipse. There's a solar eclipse when Earth moves through the moon's shadow. There's a lunar eclipse when the moon moves through Earth's shadow.

Critical Thinking

1. If Earth had two moons, would we see more lunar eclipses? Why?
2. How is a solar eclipse different from a lunar eclipse?
3. If Earth and the moon were the same size, would more people be able to see solar eclipses? Why?

WHY DOES THE MOON

CHANGE?

Night after night, the moon keeps changing. Sometimes it's full and bright. Sometimes it's half a circle. Sometimes it's only a thin slice. And sometimes you can't see it at all. In this lesson, you'll explore why the moon seems to change shape.

Minds On! A pattern is something that happens again and again. On page 15 in your *Activity Log*, make a list of things you do every day. Now, make a list of things you do every week. These lists are patterns of things that happen in your life. ●

In the activity on the next page, you'll make a model to see how Earth and the moon move together to make the pattern of change you see in the night sky.

EXPLORE Activity!

The Pattern of the Moon

If you look at the moon every night for a month, it appears to change shape. In this activity, you'll use a model to find out what's really happening.

What You Need

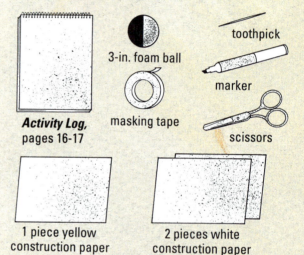

Activity Log, pages 16-17
3-in. foam ball
toothpick
masking tape
marker
scissors
1 piece yellow construction paper
2 pieces white construction paper

What To Do

1 Make a sun for your model by cutting a large circle from the yellow construction paper. Tape the sun to the middle of the front wall in your classroom. This will be the location of the sun in your model.

2 Cut each of the pieces of white construction paper into four equal squares. Label each square with a capital letter. Put A on the first square, B on the second square, and so on. Tape square A right under the sun. Tape square B in the corner of the room to the left of the sun.

Continue in that direction, taping squares C, D, and so on in the center of each wall and in each corner. When you finish, the squares should be in alphabetical order.

3 In this activity, you will be Earth. The black-and-white ball another person will hold will be the moon. Stick the toothpick into the moon anywhere that the black and white meet. Use the toothpick as a handle.

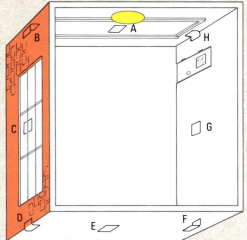

4 Have the person move the moon around Earth (you), always keeping the white side of the moon facing the sun. Observe the moon carefully as it moves around you, turning as necessary to keep the moon in sight. Observe the shape of the white part of the moon as it passes each piece of white paper.

5 Repeat step 4, changing places so that you are the moon and the other person is Earth. Compare your observations.

6 Look at the chart in your **Activity Log.** It is set up to look like the model you have made in your classroom. The circles represent the moon's orbit as it moves around Earth.

7 Repeat step 4 and draw the white part of the moon at each point of the orbit. Begin with point A, and finish with point H.

What Happened?

1. At what point could you see the most of the white part of the moon?
2. At what point could you see the least of the white part of the moon?

What Now?

1. Did the moon really change shape? Why or why not?
2. Why are we able to see only part of the moon at certain times?

EXPLORE

Moon Phases

In the Explore Activity, you saw why the moon appears to change shape. The half of the moon facing the sun is lighted. The other half is dark. That's because the moon has no light of its own. What we call moonlight is really sunlight reflected off the moon.

How much you can see depends on where the moon is in its orbit. The different amounts of the lighted side you see are called **phases** (fāz' əz).

8 From night to night, you can watch the moon become a crescent again.

9 After 29½ days, the moon is back between Earth and the sun. It's time for another new moon.

As seen from Earth

1 The phase when the moon is between Earth and the sun is called a **new moon.** You can't see the new moon because all of the side lighted by the sun faces away from Earth. There is no moonlight on those nights.

2 After three or four days, the moon has moved in its orbit so that you can see a thin sliver of the lighted side. This is a **crescent** (kres' ənt) **moon.**

3 After seven or eight days, the moon has moved one-fourth of the way around Earth. It is called a **first quarter moon.**

7 After 21 or 22 days, the moon has traveled three-fourths of the way around Earth. It only has one-fourth of the way to go, so it is called a **last quarter moon.**

6 The moon keeps moving. You see less of its lighted side.

5 After 14 or 15 days, the moon is halfway around its orbit. It is on the opposite side of Earth from the sun. Now you can see the entire lighted side of the moon. This phase is called a **full moon.**

4 As the moon orbits Earth, you can see more and more of its lighted side.

Math Link
Your Age in Orbits

The moon orbits Earth once every 29½ days. That's about once a month. How many times does the moon orbit Earth in a year? How many times has the moon orbited Earth since you were born?

TRY THIS Activity!

Mission Accomplished

What You Need
Activity Log page 18

You started Project Moonwatch at the beginning of this unit. In your **Activity Log,** you drew what the moon looked like every night. What was the moon's shape on the first night? What was its shape a week later? What was its shape at the end of the two weeks? Using what you've learned, fill in any blanks on your calendar.

Keeping Track of Time

Patterns in the sky, like moon phases and day and night, are important to living things. They are ways to keep track of time.

African white stork feeding its young

Sunrise brings daylight, and we know it's time to get up. Animals who have been sleeping begin their daily activities.

Morning-glory

Day and night are important to plants, too. During the day, green plants get energy from the sun. At night, the leaves of many plants fold, and the flowers close. This saves water, heat, and energy and gives protection from the colder night air.

Like the sun, the moon appears to rise, move across the sky, and set. Animals that you don't often see, move about and get food. They sleep during the day and are active at night. Did you know that there are some plants with flowers that open only at night?

Brown bat with prey

As the moon moves across the sky each night during the month, we observe the pattern of its phases. They have helped people keep track of time for thousands of years.

The word *moon* comes from a very old word meaning "to measure." People needed a measure of time that was longer than a day. So they used the time it takes for the moon to go through all its phases. They called that period of time a lunar month.

Clocks often showed the phases of the moon as well as the time. People wanted to know exactly when there would be a full moon. Traveling at night or getting the last of the crop harvested was easier when the moon was full.

55

The calendar in your classroom is a way to keep track of time. It's divided into months because the moon goes through its phases once every 29½ days. Did you know that both *month* and *Monday* come from the word *moon*?

For centuries, people have used the lunar calendar. It has 12 months, each with 29½ days. A lunar year has 354 days. That's the time it takes for the moon to orbit Earth 12 times.

Today, most people use the solar calendar. A solar year is 365 days, the time it takes for Earth to orbit the sun. A solar calendar has 12 months, too. But almost all the months have 30 or 31 days. Do you know which one has fewer than 30 days?

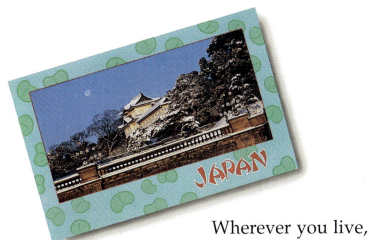

Wherever you live, you can see the moon. The moon you see is the moon that a child in Japan will see when it's night in Japan. A child in Kenya looks at the moon you'll see when it's night where you live. Knowing that makes those faraway places seem a little closer, doesn't it?

Sum It Up

For thousands of years, people used the moon to plan their lives. They made calendars, planted crops, and planned journeys based on its phases. Days, weeks, months, and years still help us organize time into a pattern that makes sense.

TRY THIS Activity!

Earth Phases?

What You Need
Materials from the Explore Activity, *Activity Log* page 19

Suppose you lived on the moon. Would Earth have phases?

Use the black-and-white ball to represent Earth. Set the classroom up with points A–H as you did in the Explore Activity. If you were on the moon at point A, what would Earth look like? Draw what you see in your ***Activity Log.*** Draw what you would see if you were on the moon at points C, D, and E. Label the drawings that represent a crescent Earth, a quarter Earth, and a full Earth.

Critical Thinking
1. During which phase of the moon would a solar eclipse or a lunar eclipse have to occur?
2. Why doesn't the sun have phases?
3. How are the moon phases different from a lunar eclipse?

Theme **T** SCALE and STRUCTURE

HOW ARE EARTH AND THE MOON DIFFERENT?

Moon's surface

Billions of people, animals, and plants live on Earth. Could they live on the moon? In this lesson, you'll explore how Earth and the moon are different. You'll also discover why we live on Earth instead of on the moon.

Minds On! Take a deep breath. Now let it out. If you were on the moon, could you do that? What about moving around? How easy would it be on the moon?

Pretend that you're going to spend a day on the moon. On page 20 in your *Activity Log,* make a list or draw what you would need to be safe there. ●

To learn what Earth is made of, scientists study its rocks, air, water, plants, and animals. One way to study the moon is to use telescopes to look at its surface. In the next activity, you'll make a model of the moon's surface.

EXPLORE Activity!

How Can You Make Moon Craters?

The surface of the moon looks very different from the surface of Earth. There are many reasons for this. One of them is the large number of craters (krā′ tərz) on the moon. Many of these craters are formed when large solid objects from space hit the moon. In this activity, you'll use a model to find out what happens to the surface of the moon when these objects hit it.

What You Need

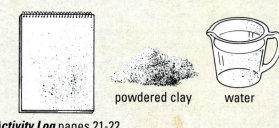

Activity Log pages 21-22

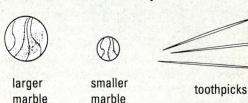

larger marble   smaller marble   toothpicks

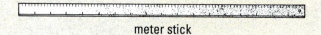
meter stick

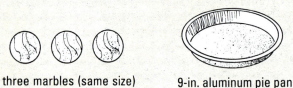

three marbles (same size)   9-in. aluminum pie pan

newspaper

safety goggles

What To Do

1. Cover a square meter area with newspaper. Place the pie pan in the center of the newspaper.

Safety!

See the *Safety Tip* in step 2.

2 ***Safety Tip:*** Put on safety goggles. Pour the clay mixture your teacher will give you into the pie pan. Smooth the surface by shaking the pan a little as it sits on the paper.

3 Use the same-sized marbles for steps 3–5. Drop a marble into the clay. Record the height from which you dropped the marble, and draw in your ***Activity Log*** what the surface looks like.

4 Repeat step 3 for each of the other marbles. Drop each of them from a different height, recording each height. Have a different group member drop each marble.

5 Using toothpicks, measure the width and depth of each crater. Record measurements in your ***Activity Log.***

What Happened?

1. What happened to the clay when the marbles hit it?
2. What are the shapes, sizes, and depths of the craters?

What Now?

1. How does the height from which each marble was dropped compare to the size and depth of the crater it made?
2. How would crater size change if you used a larger marble? How would it change if you used a smaller marble? Make a prediction. Then test it. Drop each marble from the greatest height measured in step 3 or 4.

Surface Features

In the Explore Activity, you used a model to see the way many craters on the moon were made. When one of the marbles hit the clay, part of the clay was pushed away to make room for the marble. The clay piled up in a circle with the marble in the center. The marble dropped from the greatest height made the widest crater. The bigger marble made a larger crater, while the smaller marble made a smaller crater.

Craters are hollow areas in the surface of the ground. Some craters on the moon may have been formed long ago by volcanos. But most of them were made by objects from space hitting the moon. Some craters are larger than others. The size depends on the size of the object that hit the moon in that spot. It also depends on the speed at which the object was traveling.

Large and small objects from space hit the moon's surface all the time. It is covered with craters. Earth has just a few, like this crater in Arizona.

Earth has some craters formed from volcanos like this one on an island in the South Pacific Ocean. But Earth's air protects it from almost all the objects from space. The moon has no air around it to protect it.

As objects move from space through air, it rubs against them, making them hotter and hotter. Most of them burn up before they reach Earth's surface.

SCIENCE TECHNOLOGY AND Society

Focus on Technology

Coming Home

Minds On! When two things rub against each other, it causes heat. Rub your hands together very fast. Can you feel the heat? If an object is moving fast enough, it gets hot enough to burn, even moving through air.

When a shuttle returns from space and enters the air around Earth, it's moving at a speed of more than 25,800 km (16,000 mi) per hour. It lands on the runway at a speed of 320 km (200 mi) per hour. What keeps it from burning up as it slows down? NASA designed a "skin" of 31,000 tiles to cover it. They protect it from the heat of reentry. Each one is made for an exact spot on the shuttle's belly and wings. The tiles play a big part in the shuttle's safe return.

Air and Water

Air also protects Earth from being too hot or too cold. Air reflects some of the sun's energy away from Earth during the day. At night, Earth's air acts like a blanket. Heat from Earth is trapped in the air and sent back toward Earth. Because the moon has no air, it gets much hotter and colder than Earth does. Air keeps Earth at a temperature that animals and plants can live in.

Heat

Plants need a gas called **carbon dioxide** (kär′ bon dī ok′ sīd) to make food. Plants and animals need a gas called **oxygen** (ok′ sə jən) to get energy from food. Air has these gases and others as well.

Because the moon doesn't have air, there's no carbon dioxide or oxygen for living things.

Another big difference between Earth and the moon is water. Earth has oceans of water. But the moon doesn't have a drop. The moon is drier than Earth's driest desert. Because living things need water, there is no life on the moon.

Earth has weather because of its air. The mixing of hot and cold masses of air make our weather—the rain, snow, and wind. Because the moon has no air, there is no wind.

Minds On! Between 1969 and 1972, Apollo astronauts went to the moon. They left footprints wherever they walked. On Earth, wind and water would erase them. But there's no wind or water on the moon. How long do you think the astronauts' footprints will stay there?

TRY THIS Activity!

Footprints Forever?

What You Need
clear plastic shoe box with lid, another plastic shoe box lid, mixture of sand and diatomaceous earth, rock, wooden stirrer, *Activity Log* pages 23–24

Working outdoors, pour half of the mixture into each shoe box lid. Smooth the mixture with the stirrer. Gently use your shoe to make a shoe print on each surface. Cover one lid with the plastic box and put the rock on top. This will be your moon print. Leave the other print uncovered. This will be your Earth print. Check them every day for 10 days. Record what is happening to each one and why.

Gravity

Another important difference between Earth and the moon is their gravity (grav′ i tē). **Gravity** is the pulling force between two objects. Gravity pulls you back to Earth when you jump into the air. It keeps the layer of air around Earth from moving away from Earth into space.

The moon has gravity too, but it's not as strong as Earth's. Earth's gravity is six times greater than that of the moon. The moon's gravity is too weak to "hold" a layer of air around it.

This chart shows differences between Earth and the moon. What parts have you already read about? What parts are new?

Earth and the Moon

Feature	Earth	Moon
Size (distance across)	12,756 km (7,926 mi)	3,476 km (2,160 mi)
Day length	12 hours	about 15 days
Night length	12 hours	about 15 days
Day temperature	+58°C (+136°F) Highest recorded temperature	+127°C (+260°F)
Night temperature	about −90°C (about −129°F) Lowest recorded temperature	−173°C (−280°F)
Does it have air?	Yes	No

Math  Link
What's Your Moon Weight?

How much would you weigh on the moon? It's easy to figure out. Weigh yourself at home or in the school nurse's office. Your weight will probably be in pounds. Divide your Earth weight by six to find your moon weight.

Literature  Link
The Sun

Make a Sun Chart. Working with a group, use Seymour Simon's book to find some amazing facts. After you have read it, decide what will be on your chart. Write your ideas on page 25 in your *Activity Log*. Use pictures, drawings, and words to design it. Make it as colorful as you can.

Feature	Earth	Moon
Does it have water?	Yes	No
What's it made of?	Gases, Water, Rock	Rock
Does it have soil?	Yes	No
Are there living things there?	Yes	No
Does it have craters?	Some	Thousands
Does it have gravity?	Yes	Yes
How much would the same child weigh?	66 lb	11 lb

You on the Moon

Pretend that you're standing on the surface of the moon in a space suit.

Imagine looking up, down, straight ahead, and behind you. How would what you see be different from what you see on Earth?

Sound waves are carried to your ear by the air inside your space suit. So if you whistled or said something, you could hear it. But there is no air on the moon. If you dropped something to the ground, it wouldn't make a sound.

Suppose you sprayed some perfume into the space in front of you. Could you smell it if you took off your space suit? You could, but it wouldn't be a good idea. One of the reasons you're wearing that space suit is because the moon doesn't have something you need to stay alive. What is it?

Rocks would feel the same as they do on Earth, wouldn't they? What else might you feel? Look back at the chart on page 66. What is another reason that you have to wear that space suit?

An apple would taste the same on the moon as it does on Earth. Do you know why?

Music/Art  Link
Your Own Space Suit

On page 26 in your *Activity Log*, draw a picture of a space suit you could wear on the moon. Label the parts. Tell the reason for each part. Think about all the things the suit has to do for you. It has to give you air, food, water, and a safe temperature. Share your work with the class.

 Focus on Technology

Moontown?

People may live on the moon someday. They will have to make places there as much like Earth's environment as they can. Use what you know about Earth and the moon to make plans for the first Moontown. Work with a group to decide what people will need to live and be comfortable there. Then figure out how to provide for those needs. Write your plans on page 27 in your *Activity Log*. Share your ideas with your class. Make drawings or a model to help explain your ideas.

Sum It Up

On Earth, you don't need a space suit. You have everything you need to stay alive. There's enough gravity to keep you from floating off into space. There's food, air, water, and the right temperature. The moon doesn't have what you need. To live there, you'd have to find out a way to get those things.

Critical Thinking

1. How is the soil on Earth different from the rock dust on the moon? What's in soil besides small pieces of rock?
2. Why are day and night on Earth each twelve hours long? Why is each about fifteen days long on the moon?
3. Why do rain and snow fall to the ground?

ARE THERE REASONS FOR THE

Spring, summer, fall, winter—year after year, the seasons come and go. But why do we have them? Why are they different depending on where you live?

SEASONS?

If you live in a place that's hot in the summer and cold in the winter, it's easy to see how your part of Earth changes throughout the year. If you live in a place that has two seasons instead of four, part of the year is rainy, and part is dry. A few places on Earth don't seem to have seasons at all. It's very warm, and there's plenty of rain all year round. Do you know where they are?

Minds On! On page 28 in your *Activity Log,* draw a picture that shows the seasons where you live. ●

EXPLORE Activity!

Why Is It Warmer in Summer?

You know that it's warmer in summer than in winter. Something changes as Earth revolves around the sun. In this activity, you will explore what that change is and what it has to do with seasons.

What You Need

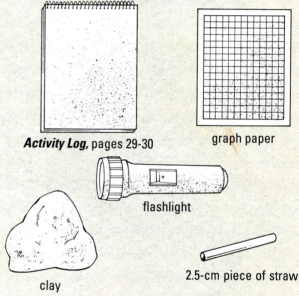

Activity Log, pages 29-30

graph paper

flashlight

clay

2.5-cm piece of straw

What To Do

1 Put the graph paper on the floor. Place the clay in the middle of the paper. Poke the straw into the clay so it stands straight up.

2 Work in a darkened room. Sit in a chair and rest your arms on your legs. Hold the flashlight, shining it straight down on the graph paper.

3 Have another person in your group trace the outline of the lighted area on the paper and count the number of squares inside the outlined area. Observe the location of the straw's shadow. Record this information in your **Activity Log.**

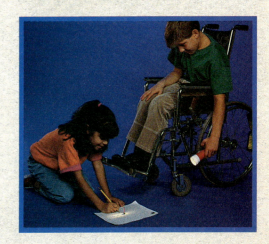

4 Now, while staying in the same place, hold the flashlight at an angle. Move the paper as necessary to get the light to shine on it. Make sure the distance from the flashlight to the paper is the same as it was in step 2.

5 Repeat step 3.

What Happened?

1. Which time were there more squares inside the outlined area?
2. Did the amount of light coming out of the flashlight change? What was it that changed?
3. Imagine the flashlight is the sun and the straw is you. Which time was the sun higher over your head? Where was the sun the other time? Which time was the sun warmer? Why?

What Now?

1. In what season of the year is the sun highest overhead at midday?
2. Which time with the flashlight and graph paper is more like winter?

EXPLORE

73

Energy From the Sun

In the Explore Activity, you saw that light shining at an angle is spread out over a larger area than when it's not shining at an angle. When the flashlight shone directly down on the paper, the light covered fewer squares. When it shone at an angle, the light covered more squares. Each of the squares in the smaller area was brighter because the light was less spread out. If you think of the flashlight as the sun and the piece of paper as Earth, it can help you understand how Earth receives energy (en' ər jē) from the sun.

Earth gets **energy** from the sun in the form of light and heat. The amount of energy that the whole Earth gets from the sun from year to year is about the same. But any one place on Earth gets different amounts of energy at different times of the year.

1 When the sun's rays shine directly on a part of Earth, the energy covers a smaller area. That means more hours of daylight, higher temperatures, and warmer weather. It's summer in North America.

direct

slanted

2 When the sun's rays slant on that same part of Earth, the energy spreads out over a bigger area. It's still the same amount of energy. It's just spread out. That means fewer hours of daylight, lower temperatures, and cooler weather. It's winter in South America.

Illustration not drawn to scale.

4 On the part of Earth tilted away from the sun, the energy is slanted and spread out. There are fewer hours of daylight, lower temperatures, and cooler weather. Now it's winter in North America.

slanted

direct

3 The sun's rays shine directly on a part of Earth sometimes and spread out at other times because Earth is tilted. It rotates at an angle as it revolves around the sun. The part of Earth tilted toward the sun gets more direct sunlight. There are more hours of daylight, higher temperatures, and warmer weather. Now it's summer in South America.

As Earth revolves around the sun, the seasons change. As a place on Earth moves away from its summer position, the hours of daylight begin to decrease, and the weather begins to get cooler. It is fall in that place. As a place on Earth moves away from its winter position, the hours of daylight begin to increase, and the weather begins to get warmer. It is spring in that place.

Where Is It Summer?

What You Need
globe, flashlight

Notice that the globe is tilted, just like Earth. Find the line around the middle of the globe. It's called the equator (i kwā′ tər). The **equator** is an imaginary line that divides Earth into a top and a bottom half. These halves are called **hemispheres** (hem′ i sfîrz). Now find the North Pole and the South Pole. If the North Pole is pointed toward the sun, the South Pole is pointed away. The Northern Hemisphere of Earth is having summer, and the Southern Hemisphere is having winter.

Turn the globe so that the United States is in front of you. Hold a flashlight over the U.S. Pretend that the flashlight is the sun. Hold it steady as you slowly spin the globe with your other hand. Have a partner call out the countries that are also lit by the flashlight. These places have summer at the same time.

How Many Hours?

What You Need
globe, flashlight, marker, string, scissors, tape

Work in a darkened room. Have partners help you position the globe and flashlight so that Earth is tilted exactly as on page 74.

Choose a city on the globe. Imagine a straight line that goes around the Earth starting and ending at this city. Attach string here, then rotate the globe keeping the string on the imaginary line. When you complete a rotation, cut and tape the string to the globe. Again rotate the globe, this time coloring the string from where your city passes into darkness until it passes back into light. This colored section of string represents night, the uncolored section day. Remove the string.

Have partners help you position the globe and flashlight so that Earth is tilted exactly as on page 75. Repeat activity using the same city.

Which string shows the daylight hours of summer? Which string shows the daylight hours of winter? How do you know? How might the strings of other cities compare? Share results.

Sun Power

The sun's energy and the angle at which this energy shines on Earth cause the seasons. Living things have life cycles that are connected to the place where they live. Plants change with the seasons. In some places, the changes are easy to see. Some trees that grow where winters are cold lose their leaves and stop growing. They grow new ones in the spring that grow all summer.

Life cycles of animals are connected to seasons. Some who live where winters are cold grow thick coats. They shed them for lighter coats in summer. Others leave and come back when winter is over. Still others sleep through the winter.

Is your life connected to the seasons? Let's see. Do you live in a place where you wear warmer clothes during part of the year? Do you heat your home during a certain time of the year? Is it sometimes too hot, too cold, or too wet to do what you'd like to do? If you answered *yes* to any of these questions, the seasons have an effect on your life.

Snowshoe hare

Summer

Winter

Health Link **Watch Out for UV!**

Is the sun's energy dangerous? It can be. Part of it is called **ultraviolet** (ul′ trə vī′ ə lit) **light (UV)**. It's what causes you to get a suntan or sunburn. Too much can even cause skin cancer. That's why you should protect your skin from too much sun. Find out more about this by interviewing 10 people. Ask each one how he or she protects against too much sun. Write what they tell you on page 31 in your *Activity Log*. Share the results of your poll with your class.

Some creams protect against UV.

Pollution-producing factories

SCIENCE TECHNOLOGY and Society

Focus on Environment

Taking Care of Earth

Energy from the sun is clean. You know that burning coal and gasoline to get energy causes pollution. Here are some ways to use the sun's energy more. Houses and other buildings that are built with large windows facing the south can trap more of the sun's energy. They need less fuel to heat them. Many machines can be powered by solar energy. Refrigerators, water heaters, TV sets, and cooking stoves are some of them.

Cars, boats, and airplanes can also be powered by solar cells. These vehicles cause no pollution. And solar cells really work well to power spacecraft in space. Do you know why?

Solar car

Solar telephone

Telephones can run on solar energy, too. A panel containing solar cells collects and stores the sun's energy. **Solar cells** capture the rays of the sun and turn them directly into electricity.

Sum It Up

Almost all life depends on energy from the sun. That energy is in the form of light and heat. The total amount of energy that Earth gets from year to year is about the same. But parts of Earth get different amounts of energy during the year depending on if that part is tilted toward or away from the sun. That's what causes the seasons.

Critical Thinking

1. What would happen to the seasons if Earth weren't tilted?
2. If you lived near the equator, would it be hot most of the time or cold most the time? Why?
3. Why do you think there are different time zones in large countries?

Theme T SYSTEMS and INTERACTIONS

Your Solar Neighborhood

In a way, you are coming to the end of a journey that has taken you out into space for a closer look at the sun, Earth, and the moon. You've seen that they are part of a system. The way the system works makes night and day, seasons, moon phases, and eclipses. The system helps you understand your place in space.

In the book *My Place in Space*, Henry Wilson knew exactly where he lived. If he had written it on an envelope, it would have looked like this.

Henry Wilson
12 Main Street
Gumbridge, Australia
Southern Hemisphere
Planet Earth
Solar System
The Milky Way Galaxy

The sun, Earth, and the moon are part of a larger system called the **Solar System**. The sun is its center. There are other planets besides Earth. Do you know any of their names? Some of the planets have moons. Besides the sun, the planets, and their moons, there are other large and small objects in the Solar System. You may know them as comets (kom' itz), asteroids (as' tə roidz'), and space dust.

Henry's long address tells you more about his place in space. It's your place, too.

Everything in the Solar System orbits the sun. The sun's gravity is so strong, it holds the whole Solar System in place. The sun is also the source of light. Without it, the Solar System would have almost no light and little heat.

Our Solar System is part of an even larger system called the **Milky Way Galaxy** (gal' ək sē). There are billions of stars in it. Our sun is one of them.

Now that you know even more about your place in space, write your address on page 32 in your *Activity Log*. How is it like Henry Wilson's address? How is it different? You might want to make up your own story about your place in space. In the next activity, you'll find out how to make shadow puppets. You can use them in a shadow theater to tell many different stories.

Literature  Link

Shadow Puppets

In this activity, you can use shadows to help you tell a story. You will need a white sheet hung across a wire, a light source, a large cardboard box, scissors, construction paper, a pen, some craft sticks, and masking tape.

You and your friends can make a play about the story *My Place in Space* or *The Truth About the Moon* with shadow puppets in a shadow theater.

First, read the book again to decide who the characters in your play will be. Next, plan what each of the characters in your play will say. Write your plans on page 33 in your **Activity Log.** Then, make a shadow puppet for each character. Use your puppets to act out the story for the rest of your class.

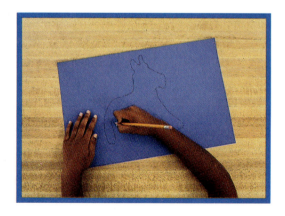

To make the puppets, draw the shape of each character from the book on construction paper.

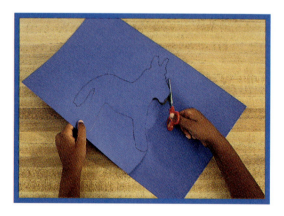

Next, carefully cut around each shape.

Then, tape each character to the end of a craft stick.

Your classmates will see the shadows your puppets are casting on the sheet.

Now, get the theater ready. Hang the sheet across a wire. Use the box for the "stage." The sheet should be in front of it. Have your audience sit in front of the sheet. You, the stage, your puppets, and your light should be on the other side of the sheet. Darken the room. Turn on your light. Get behind the stage so that you (and your shadows) can't be seen. Begin by raising the first puppet up above the stage. Your shadow play has begun.

GLOSSARY

Use the pronunciation key below to help you decode, or read, the pronunciations.

Pronunciation Key

a	at, bad	d	dear, soda, bad
ā	ape, pain, day, break	f	five, defend, leaf, off, cough, elephant
ä	father, car, heart	g	game, ago, fog, egg
âr	care, pair, bear, their, where	h	hat, ahead
e	end, pet, said, heaven, friend	hw	white, whether, which
ē	equal, me, feet, team, piece, key	j	joke, enjoy, gem, page, edge
i	it, big, English, hymn	k	kite, bakery, seek, tack, cat
ī	ice, fine, lie, my	l	lid, sailor, feel, ball, allow
îr	ear, deer, here, pierce	m	man, family, dream
o	odd, hot, watch	n	not, final, pan, knife
ō	old, oat, toe, low	ng	long, singer, pink
ô	coffee, all, taught, law, fought	p	pail, repair, soap, happy
ôr	order, fork, horse, story, pour	r	ride, parent, wear, more, marry
oi	oil, toy	s	sit, aside, pets, cent, pass
ou	out, now	sh	shoe, washer, fish mission, nation
u	up, mud, love, double	t	tag, pretend, fat, button, dressed
ū	use, mule, cue, feud, few	th	thin, panther, both
ü	rule, true, food	<u>th</u>	this, mother, smooth
ů	put, wood, should	v	very, favor, wave
ûr	burn, hurry, term, bird, word, courage	w	wet, weather, reward
ə	about, taken, pencil, lemon, circus	y	yes, onion
b	bat, above, job	z	zoo, lazy, jazz, rose, dogs, houses
ch	chin, such, match	zh	vision, treasure, seizure

asteroids (as´tə roidz) little, rocky planets that orbit the sun, mostly between Mars and Jupiter

astronomers (ə stron´ ə mərz) scientists who study the sun, moon, planets, stars, and other objects in the sky

binoculars (bə nok´yə lərz) a hand-held instrument consisting of two small telescopes joined together, used to view far-off objects

carbon dioxide (kär´ bən dī ok´sīd) a colorless, odorless gas, made up of carbon and oxygen, that is present in the atmosphere. Carbon dioxide is exhaled by animals as a waste product and used by plants to make food.

comets (kom´ itz) objects in space made of frozen gases, rock pieces, and dust. They orbit the sun in long, narrow orbits.

crater (krā´tər) a hollowed area on the surface of the ground

crescent moon (kres´ənt) a phase of the moon that occurs several days after a new moon or several days before the next new moon

eclipse (i klips´) a partial or total darkening or hiding of the sun, the moon, or a planet

84

energy (en´ər jē) the ability to make things move, heat up, or to cause other changes in matter. Earth gets energy from the sun in the form of light and heat.

equator (i kwā´ tər) an imaginary line that circles Earth halfway between the North and South Poles.

first quarter moon a phase of the moon that is visible about 7 days after the new moon

full moon a phase of the moon in which you can see all the lighted side of the moon

gravity (grav´i tē) the pulling force between two objects

hemisphere (hem´i sfîr) half of a sphere or globe. The globe is divided into northern and southern hemispheres by the equator.

last quarter moon a phase of the moon that is visible about 22 days after new moon

lenses (len´səz) pieces of glass or other transparent material, that have one or both surfaces curved. This causes the image passing through them to be enlarged or reduced.

lunar eclipse (lü´nər i klips´) a partial or total darkening of the moon caused when the moon passes through Earth's shadow

Milky Way Galaxy (gal´ək sē) a system of stars, gases, and dust, appearing as a bright white path across the sky. Our solar system is part of the Milky Way Galaxy.

new moon a phase of the moon in which all of the lighted side faces away from Earth

observatory (əb zûr´və tor´ē) building where astronomers use instruments to observe and study objects in the sky

orbit (ôr´ bit) the path an object follows when it revolves around another object

oxygen (ok´sə jən) a colorless, odorless gas found in the air. Oxygen is essential to life.

phases (fāz´əz) the changing appearance of the moon at a particular time, depending on how much of its lighted side can be seen from Earth

revolve (ri volv´) to move around another object. Earth revolves around the sun.

rotate (rō´tāt) to spin. Earth rotates once in each 24-hour day.

skyglow (skī´glō) brightness produced by thousands of city lights that makes it difficult to view objects in outer space

solar cell (sō´lər sel) a device that changes the sun's energy to electricity

solar eclipse (sō´lər i klips´) a partial or total darkening of the sun caused when the moon moves between Earth and the sun

solar system (sō´lər sis´təm) the name for our sun and all the space objects traveling around it

system (sis´təm) a group of objects combined to form a whole and to move or work together

telescope (tel´ə skōp´) an instrument used to view faraway objects that makes them look closer and clearer

ultraviolet (ul´trə vī´ ə lit) **light** invisible rays of light present in sunlight that can be dangerous to the skin

INDEX

Air, 63-66, 68
Al-Battani, 19
Animals, 44, 54, 64, 77
Animators, 24
Aryabhata the First, 18
Asteroids, 80
Astronauts, 65; *illus.*, 9
Astronomers, 13, 16, 18-19, 22, 24-25, 45-46

Bess, Clayton, 10
Binoculars, 23-24; *act.*, 23; *illus.*, 23
Book reviews, 10-11

Calendar, 17, 56
Carbon dioxide, 64-65
Clocks, 47, 55
Comets, 80
Copernicus, Nicolaus, 19
Craters, 60, 62; *act.*, 60-61; *illus.*, 62-63
Crescent moon, 52; *illus.*, 52

Day and night, 16-17, 21, 54; *act.*, 14-15, 21, 76; *illus.*, 16-17

Earth, 64-65; *table,* 66-67; air, 63-64; craters, 63; *illus.*, 63; distance, 30, 32-33, 42; *act.*, 33; movement, 16-21; *act.*, 14-15; phases *act.*, 57; seasons, 71, 74-75, 77; *act.*, 72-73, 76; *illus.*, 74-75; shadow, 40-41, 43; *act.*, 38-39; size, 30-31, 35; *act.*, 31; *illus.*, 30
Eclipse, 41, 43, 46; *act.*, 38-39; *illus.*, 41-45; lunar, 40-41; partial, 44-45; solar, 42-43; total, 44-45
Energy, 74-75, 77-78
Equator, 76
Eyepiece, *illus.*, 22

First quarter moon, 52; *illus.*, 52
Footprints, 65; *act.*, 65
Full moon, 34, 53, 55; *illus.*, 53

Galileo, 19-20, 22
Gravity, 66-67, 81

Hemisphere, 76
Hypatia, 18

Jupiter, 20

Last quarter moon, 53; *illus.*, 53

Lenses, 22-23
Life cycles, 77
Light, 22-23, 32, 74-76, 81
Light pollution, 25
Lunar calendar, 56
Lunar eclipse, 40-41, 43, 45
Lunar month, 55-56
Lunar year, 56

Milky Way Galaxy, 81; *illus.*, 81
Models, 14, 24
Month, 56
Moon, 10, 55-57, 64-69; *table,* 66-67; craters, 62; *act.*, 60-61; distance, 30, 32-33, 42; *act.*, 33; movement, 16-20, 56; *illus.*, 52-53; phases, 52, 55; *act.*, 9, 50-51, 53; *illus.*, 52-53; shadow, 40-44; *act.*, 38-39; size, 27, 30-35, 42; *act.*, 28-29, 31, 34; *illus.*, 30. *See also* Lunar calendar; Lunar eclipse
Moonlight, 32, 52
Moonprint, 65; *act.*, 65
Moontown, 69
My Place in Space **(Hirst and Hirst),** 11, 80

New moon, 52; *illus.*, 52
Night, 16-17, 25. *See also* Day and night

North Pole, 76

Observatories, 17; *illus.,* 46
Orbit, 20, 43, 52-53, 81; *illus.,* 20-21, 56. *See also* Revolution
Orphan Boy, The **(Mollel),** 11
Oxygen, 64-65

Partial eclipse, 45
Pattern, 49
Phases, 52
Phases, earth, *act.,* 57
Phases, moon, 52-53, 55, 56, 57; *act.,* 50-51; *illus.,* 52-53
Plants, 54, 64, 77
Pollution, 25, 78-79
Project Moonwatch, 53; *act.,* 9, 53
Ptolemy, 18

Revolution, 17-21. *See also* Orbit
Rotation, 16-19, 21, 47, 75

Scientists, 8-9, 46
Seasons, 11, 19, 71, 76; *act.,* 72-73, 76; *illus.,* 74-75, 77
Shadows, 36, 40-44, 47; *act.,* 38-39, 82

Shadow puppets, 82-83; *act.,* 82-83; *illus.,* 83
Shadow sticks, 47
Shadow theater, 82, *illus.,* 83
Shuttle, the, 63
Simon, Seymour, 11, 67
Size, 27, 30-31; *act.,* 28-29, 31, 34, 35; *illus.,* 32
Skin cancer, 78
Skyglow, 24-25; *illus.,* 25
Solar calendar, 56
Solar cells, 79; *illus.,* 79
Solar eclipse, 42-46; *illus.,* 42-43, 44-45
Solar energy, 74-75, 77-79
Solar system, 11, 80-81; *illus.,* 80-81
Solar year, 56
South Pole, 76
Space dust, 80
Space suit, 68-69; *illus.,* 68
Stars, 25, 81
Stone Patterns, *illus.,* 17
Sun, 11, 16, 81; *act.,* 14-15, 38-39, 45; distance, 30, 32-33; *act.,* 33; energy, 74-75, 77-79; movement, 17-18; size, 27, 30-33, 35; *act.,* 28-29, 31; *illus.,* 30. *See also* Solar calendar; Solar cells; Solar eclipse
Sun, The **(Simon)** 11, 67
Sundial, 47; *illus.,* 47

Sun-earth-moon system, 20-22, 32-33, 38-39, 56, 80-81; *act.,* 33; *illus.,* 56, 80-81
Sunlight, 32, 52
Sunshine Makes the Seasons **(Branley),** 11
Suntan/sunburn, 78
Sun viewer, *act.,* 45
System, 8; *illus.,* 8

Telescopes, 9, 19-20, 22-24, 59; *illus.,* 22-23
Time, 47, 54-56
Total eclipse, 45
Tripod, *illus.,* 22
Truth About the Moon, The **(Bess),** 10, 82

Ultraviolet light (UV), 78

Volcanoes, 62-63

Water, 65
Weather, 65, 75; *act.,* 65. *See also* Seasons

Year, 19-20

Zhou Yue, 18

CREDITS

Photo Credits:
Cover, The Image Bank/Steven Hunt; **2, 3,** Daryl Benson/Masterfile; **3,** ©KS Studios/1991; **6,** NASA; **6, 7,** NASA; **7,** ©Comstock Inc.; **8,** ©KS Studios/1991; **9,** (l) The Image Bank, (r) The Bettman Archive; **11,** ©Studiohio; **12, 13,** The Image Bank/ Al Satterwhite; **14, 15,** ©KS Studios/1991; **17,** ©L.H. Robbins; **22, 23,** ©KS Studios/1991; **24,** ©Brent Turner/BLT Productions/1991; **25,** The Image Bank/Don Carroll; **26, 27,** The Image Bank/Steve Dunwell; **28, 29,** Ken Karp for MMSD; **30,** (l) Tom Stack/Tom Stack & Associates, (r) Shattil/Rozinski/Tom Stack & Associates; **34,** ©Earth Scenes/Charlie Palek; **35,** ©Earth Scenes/Joe McDonald; **36, 37, 38, 39,** ©KS Studios/1991; **43,** The Image Bank/JoAnna McCarthy; **44,** ©Stephen Dalton, Science Source/Photo Researchers; **46,** (tl) Print Collection, Miriam & Ira D. Wallach, Division of Art, Prints & Photographs, The New York Public Library, Aftor, Lennox and Tilden Foundations, (mr) The Image Bank/Miguel, (ml) ©Philip Rosenberg Photography/1991, (br) ©Doug Martin; **47,** ©Eunice Harris/Photo Researchers; **48, 49,** Daryl Benson/Masterfile; **50, 51,** ©Doug Martin; **54,** (t) Animals Animals/Robert Maier, (m) Tom Evans/Photo Researchers, (b) ©Merlin D. Tuttle/The National Audubon Society Collection/Photo Researchers; **55,** ©Joe Pospisil/Painted Elephant Productions/1991; **57,** (t) TravelPix/FPG International, (b) ©G. Planchenault/Agence Vandystadt/Photo Researchers; **58,** NASA; **58, 59,** Darlene Murawski/Tony Stone Worldwide/Chicago Ltd.; **61,** ©KS Studios/1991; **62, 63,** NASA; **62,** (b) ©François Gohier, Science Source/Photo Researchers; **63,** (t) The Image Bank/Larry Dale Gorden, (b) Yerkes Observatory; **65,** NASA; **68,** ©KS Studios/1991/suit courtesy of U.S. Space Camp®; **70, 71,** ©Comstock Inc.; **73,** Ken Karp for MMSD; **77,** (tl) The Image Bank/John & Martha Stradiotto, (tr) ©Tom & Pat Leeson, Science Source/Photo Researchers, (bl) (br), ©KS Studios/1991; **78,** (t) ©KS Studios/1991, (b) The Image Bank/Murray Alcosser; **79,** (t) Greg Vaughn/Tom Stack & Associates, (b) ©François Gohier, Science Source/Photo Researchers; **81,** ©Fred Espenak, Science Source/Photo Researchers; **82, 83,** ©KS Studios/1991.

Illustration Credits:
 6, 7, Evangelia Philippidis/Bob James; **14, 28, 38, 50, 60, 72,** Bob Giuliani; **16, 17, 20, 21, 30-33, 40-45, 52, 53, 56, 74, 75,** Gary Ciccarelli; **18, 19,** Richard Cowdrey; **51,** James Shough; **57,** Jim Theodore; **64, 65,** Jan Willis